Norah the Polar
& Marcin, the Polar Bear Whisperer

A story about hope, friendship and solutions
for taking care of the Earth

WRITTEN BY CLAUDIA VAN ZUIDEN

Norah the Polar Bear & Marcin, the Polar Bear Whisperer

ISBN: 978-90-8324-490-7
Illustrations: Brenda Higgins
Author's website: www.solutionways.com
Layout Design: Shazeb Khan

'Norah the Polar Bear' is a beautifully written story about how climate change is impacting our world today. However, it is much more than that. Woven throughout the story you will learn about solution focused thinking and skills, resilience, the benefits of living in a mindful way, the importance of 'being' rather than 'doing' and how everything is always changing.

As a former teacher and head teacher, I believe this would make a very good book study for a class. The discussion points at the end of the story provide many opportunities for further learning.

As a Granny to a growing brood of grandchildren, I think it would be a lovely book to snuggle up with, to nurture an interest in the ever changing world that we are living in today. Our grandchildren are our future!" - Gillian Watt, Former Headteacher Monymask Primary School, Founder AndBreathe, Scotland, UK

"I love the book! I am in awe at how many important messages and themes you managed to cram into it whilst still keeping the overall feeling simple and uncluttered. The characters are endearing. I love it's positivity. My instant reaction was that I wanted to share it with all my colleagues and shout "Read this to your class!" As well as being what children need to hear and discuss, it hits LOTS of outcomes on the curriculum. I will wait until it is published then recommend it to everyone.

Your book was an absolute hit with the children. They love Norah. We read the story in two parts. I then gave the children little pieces of paper to write down their very first thoughts after listening to it and what they would like to say to you. The children, I think, have fallen in love with you through your words. They were full of encouragement and want you to write more stories. You will love reading their comments.

They are so excited about it all. You and your book have really captured their imagination.

I wish you lots of success with your book. It really is wonderful. I'm not saying that because I want to make you happy, it genuinely is amazing. I know lots of teachers who are looking for a positive way to engage children in learning about climate change and you have created it.

This uplifting book provides a refreshingly positive approach to addressing the challenges of climate change with children, in a way that is filled with inspiration and hope. Claudia's captivating characters instantly befriend the reader, opening their eyes and hearts to the wonders of the world. Their friendship creates a strong space where children can feel safe in the knowledge that they can dream big and find solutions to the challenges facing our natural world. This is the book those working with young children have been yearning for. Not only does it tackle the complex topic of climate change in a way that is pro-active and filled with hope, it quietly teaches children valuable skills and attributes to support them in achieving their dreams. Every classroom should have a copy of this book. It is sure to become a well-thumbed favourite tale as Norah and Marcin settle themselves in the hearts of children around this beautiful world." - Lorna Lees, Primary School Teacher, Scotland, UK

"Reading this book transported me to a place of wonder. Thank you for writing this lovely story. I really appreciated the themes of relocation and isolation and what it means to belong, gently illustrating how we can adjust to new ways of being and respond to our new environment in positive ways when we least expect it. Sometimes the connections we find with beings different from ourselves are surprising. This tale uses the innocence of childhood and a pure desire to bond to make even the most unlikely interactions possible." - Magi Winmill-Hermann, UK

"I loved the book. It is so good that you love animals. And please can you write a part 2?" - Isla, age 8, Scotland, UK

"I loved your book, it was amazing. Next time can you make another book because it was good and if you have Teams, you can call the teacher and read the book to us please?" - Alexis, age 9, Scotland, UK

"Dear Claudia, I think your story is very good. I think you should keep writing stories as it was amazing." - Leah, age 7, Scotland, UK

"The story is brilliant. You should keep writing stories." - Louise, age 7, Scotland, UK

"The book was so good. I felt happy about that book." - Donald, age 7, Scotland, UK

"The book was amazing. The best I ever I read." - Jack, age 8, Scotland, UK

"Dear Claudia, I loved the story. I think children will love it." - Lexi, age 8, Scotland, UK

"That was brill! Keep on writing more stories!" - Dylan, age 8, Scotland, UK

"Claudia, kids should hear this." - Adam, age 7, Scotland, UK

"Dear Claudia, I loved your book. I want to buy it." - Alfie, age 9, Scotland, UK

CONTENTS

Acknowledgement & Dedication

This book is dedicated to my three children, Daniel, Dominique and Pema, who are my greatest teachers in life and inspire me daily with their limitless, unconditional love and joy. With deep gratitude also for my parents and grandparents who showed such great care for me, and who supported me to follow my dreams. To my grandson, Nema, who lights up this world so much already. And to the love of my life, Arturo, who continues to show me the path to the heart and how to follow my dreams, which includes writing. To my friends who encouraged me and supported me to publish this book.

To Nina Eggens, for her editing skills and to Alexandra van Rijen, for the final editing and for her limitless love as a friend.

For Brenda Higgins' illustrations, who was able to capture the love between Norah and Marcin perfectly. To Steve Smith, my former colleague and lecturer in Solution Focused Brief Therapy at Robert Gordon University, Aberdeen, Scotland, who endlessly supported me to travel the world and spread the benefits of the Solution Focused Approach. To Sujen Maharjan, former President of the Central Association of Psychology Students at Tribhuvan University, Kathmandu, Nepal for inviting me to teach SFBT skills in Nepal and to all the students who took the next steps to empowerment in their own communities after their training in SFBT techniques.

To the students in the African continent, such as Zimbabwe, Kenya, Tanzania and Uganda who also have taken the SFBT skills in their communities, such as in the Joedy Foundation. To my colleague Thabisani Ncube, who takes SFBT techniques in the African Continent to the next level.

To Magi Winmill-Hermann and Gillian Watt, who proof-read this book and encouraged me to publish the book. To Lorna Lees for reading the book with the pupils of her class and for urging me to share the story of Norah with the world.

To Shazeb Khan for his creativity and endless patience with the design of the lay-out.

To my daughter Dominique, for the final editing, for her creativity and her valuable advice.

To all the children of Lorna's class in Scotland, UK, whose letters and pictures I received with such gratitude. Your enthusiasm was so contagious, thank you for your amazing feedback and for the love for Norah, Marcin and the Planet.

And last but certainly not least, to my dear, late, friend Greta Huuva, Sami Medicine Woman, who so kindly took me under her wing and shared with me the Bear Saga and stories about the beautiful bears and why we should respect them so much.

May you all be well, may you all be happy, may you all be safe & may your heart be your North Star, wherever you are.

Chapter 1
Norah, the Bear from the North

Let me tell you a story - a story that I heard from someone who heard it from someone. It is a story about a polar bear whose name is Norah and a boy called Marcin.

Once upon a time - actually not that very long ago, there was a bear who lived in a lush, green place with lots of trees, called a wildlife park, or a 'zoo'. The bear's name was Norah and she had beautiful white fur. This was quite unusual, as most bears in the wildlife park had brown or black fur. You see, Norah didn't really belong to the place she now lived in. Norah had settled in this zoo, quite a few seasons ago, after she had travelled a long way. Before she came to live at the zoo, Norah used to live in a place called 'the North Pole'. Just like her mother and her grandmother, she was born there and it was her home.

Norah used to live a great life at the North Pole. She loved the seasons there; some were really sunny and warm, and there were times when the temperature was extremely cold. There were also times when there was hardly any day-light at all, which made it very difficult to tell if it was daytime or nighttime. When it was really cold, everything outside became frozen and got covered with a blanket of snow. If it wasn't for Norah's round, black nose and her very dark brown eyes, you would not be able to notice her in that sparkly, snow-covered place. Her beautiful fur coat was like camouflage in the white snowy landscape that went on for miles and miles.

At other times, the sky would be covered with rays of light, called the 'Northern Lights' or Aurora Borealis. Rays of vibrant blues, greens, violets and pinks made it look like the sky was dancing. And if you listened very carefully, you could even hear the sky sparkle, like there was a lot of electricity in the air. Some bears would say that it almost sounded like the sky was singing when the Northern Lights came out.

Norah would often sit quietly, in complete awe, gazing at those magical lights. She would find herself wondering and pondering about these amazing wonders of nature, for a very long time.

Every so often, whilst she was gazing, she would nod off into a very peaceful dreamlike state. Regularly, she would find herself suddenly waking up, realising that she had fallen over to her side, and that she had landed on the fluffy, sparkling snow.

One of those times when she gently pushed herself up and shook the snow off her white furry body, she looked up and saw that all the colours in the sky had totally disappeared. She could hardly believe they had gone and wondered if she had been dreaming. It did not really matter much if she had imagined that those lights had been out or not. Being out in the frost, under those clear and super bright stars that were shining down on the pure, white snow, was a magical and special experience every time on its own.

Life at the North Pole was exciting, and Norah had to be brave and strong to live there. Sometimes it was so cold, that the lakes and even the sea would be frozen with a very thick layer of ice. Luckily, Norah's dense and silky white fur coat protected her very well from the cold temperatures. But, the thick layer of ice made it often very difficult for Norah to catch fish for her meals. She then really had to work hard before she found something to eat. She would have to bounce on the ice for hours, with her full body weight, for it to crack open a bit. The crack would then create a hole in the ice where Norah could go underneath into the water and search for food.

Sometimes she would be lucky and catch a very large fish, which was enough for breakfast, lunch and dinner all at once. Norah absolutely loved going fishing - she always felt that it was like going on an exciting adventure. She loved swimming in the sea to look for food - just to explore where the best areas were, and to find enough food that could last her for a few days. Both fishing and eating made her feel happy and she would always have an excellent sleep after all those efforts in finding a meal. When she was lucky enough to find a meal, her tummy would feel full, her body would feel refreshed by the cold water of the sea and she would feel totally nourished.

Although Norah loved those cold day's adventures, she also loved the days when it was warmer. The feeling of the hot sun warming up her whole body, filled her with joy too. Sometimes, in those summer months, she would feel so hot in her thick white coat that she had to jump into the sea to cool herself down. The water that was still very cold, always felt so super refreshing then. Even though her fur coat would get thinner in the summer months, it was still not easy to cool down in very hot weather, even after a swim.

However, Norah was always able to find solutions whenever things were difficult or challenging. So instead of going for a swim when she was feeling too hot, Norah would sometimes decide to just lay still for a few hours in the shade of a big boulder. She would lay there until the sun had gone down a little and the heat would be less intense. You could say that she was doing 'nothing'. However, doing 'nothing' whilst laying in the shade was the perfect solution to her problem. Norah liked it very much when solutions came so easy to her like that, as bears love to do just absolutely nothing sometimes.

Chapter 2
Learning from others and finding solutions

Finding solutions came naturally to Norah - she always seemed to solve problems quite easily in her life, whether it was trying to find food or trying to stay cool. Most bears on the North Pole live on their own. Just like them, Norah had to be strong and resilient and rely on herself most of the time. Usually, there would be nobody else nearby to help her. On the rare occasion that Norah would meet other bears, she would watch from a distance and learn from them how they caught their fish, how they stayed cool and some other things bears do to survive. She learned a lot from just observing all their skills.

There were also a lot of skills that Norah remembered which her mum had taught her. Her mum had shown her how to find food and how to check if the ice was strong enough to stand on so it could hold her weight. She had also taught Norah how to break the ice to find food, how to use her energy wisely and not to waste it. This was really important to know, especially when she could not find food easily when much water was frozen for a very long time.

Norah also had many happy memories of the times when the days were warmer and when the snow and ice had totally disappeared. The ground would be mostly green in colour, because it was covered by lush grass. Some parts would be mixed with the most beautiful, delicate, colourful flowers, such as bright purple, pink and yellow. She loved the smell of all the flowers. She sometimes used to lay down on the ground and would put her big black, shiny nose on the grass causing the subtle fragrances of the flowers to reach her nostrils. She could smell their delicate sweetness well like this. The scent, together with the tiny flower petals tickling the tip of her nostrils, often made Norah sneeze so hard that she would give herself an immense fright as it was so loud! She had to laugh afterwards of course, as sneezing is nothing to be scared about.

Norah loved looking at the butterflies too. They created a wonderful display of colours, patterns and shapes. There was such a variety of them; some very small ones and quite big ones too. They danced and danced and flew around in the sky and sometimes would land on flowers or stones. Norah would try to 'follow' the butterflies' movements with her eyes, but would get so dizzy that she occasionally would tumble over, landing on her back with all four paws up in the air. This 'Butterflies Dance', as she used to call it, reminded her of the 'Dancing Sky Lights'. Those vibrant coloured lights she would watch on the days when the green grass was covered by a blanket of snow.

When Norah would look down at her own fur, she would see that it was mostly, one colour only- it was white like the snow and the ice. But, some patches on her fur were darker in colour than other parts, such as the parts near her toes. There were more animals, such as the snow hare, who were mostly white in colour, like Norah herself. But Norah had observed something extra-ordinary; these hares could change the colour of their fur, depending on the different seasons. "That is a pretty impressive skill to have!", Norah thought to herself, as she realized that this changing of colour', makes the hares almost look invisible to predators and therefore keeps them safer.

Chapter 3
If everything changes, everything is possible

Most of us know that in Life, everything changes all the time and nothing stays exactly the same. Day becomes night, summer becomes winter, temperatures change and butterflies come and go. Norah knew this very well. For example, she had never seen butterflies flying around when everything was covered with snow and ice. She had only seen them when the fields were green and the days were warm.

She had also noticed that some days it rained, or it could be sunny and dry on the same day, and on other days the sky was just covered with clouds. Even the clouds changed; they could look grey; they could look nearly black or they could be all joined together and look like a big white blanket. Sometimes they looked like white fluffy bits, similar as those you find on the cotton grass flowers. Nothing was ever exactly as it had been before.

The sea was also always different. It could be frozen or it could have different colours. It could have massive waves or be so still that when Norah put one of her paws in, small circles would become big circles and they would ripple out so wide that she could see them floating out towards the horizon. Norah had accepted that things change all the time. She knew to enjoy the fun things that would happen and to accept certain things she could not change, such as the weather. If she could change it, she would do something about it.

Birds were some of Norah's best friends. Norah loved all the birds that came to the place where she lived, when the warmer days came. The birds had so many different colours and shapes. Norah knew that when some of these birds would fly above her in the skies, the ice would start to melt pretty soon and the days would be getting longer and warmer. She also knew that it would get colder again when those birds were not flying in the skies anymore and that their babies had grown into large birds. As soon as the days got shorter and cooler, different types of birds would fly in the sky instead.

This is how Norah knew that everything changes all the time, just by noticing the things around, below and above her. Noticing all this, helped her to understand that when life was difficult, such as when she could not find food or she felt very tired, it would not be like that forever. Realising this, Norah would get a feeling of hope, knowing that it could get better. She would ask herself what she could do, even if it was just a small thing, that could make her feel better in the meantime, until she had found a solution for the problem.

There had been a few times when Norah felt very hungry because of not having food for a while. Once, it had been really cold for a very long period of time. She had looked everywhere for food. For many days she could not find anything to eat. In the far distance, she could see those grey clouds coming closer and closer towards her and she knew that those types of clouds would bring a massive snow storm.

As she was still feeling really hungry, she knew that it was impossible to continue to try and find food whenever the snow storm would arrive. The snow would soon be falling all around her, preventing her to see far distances. Norah decided at that time, that it would be best to stay calm and look for a shelter from the storm. Pretty soon Norah managed to find a place to hide. The place she found, was a covered space hidden inside a few massive rocks. The rocks were mostly covered in ice and snow, which made the shelter look like a small cave. Norah was still very hungry, but knew that continuing to hunt for food meant she would only exhaust herself. It would mean that she would use most of the little energy she had left in her body. She decided to save her energy for now and look further for food when the storm had passed. She felt that was the best solution for that moment.

Although she didn't solve the problem of feeling hungry and feeding herself, at least she didn't make herself even more tired than she already was.

When the winter was harsh and food supplies were low, Norah had learned how to preserve her energy levels well. She was able to use some of the lessons she had learned, in other situations too. Some of these lessons helped Norah to adapt easier to the new environment where she found herself in now. Her new home was a wildlife park, situated in a lush green forest. This place was so incredibly different from the beautiful North Pole, where she used to live. She really had to learn to adapt to living in this new environment. She could often be seen pondering on a rock, where she would sit quietly, trying to find solutions to her new challenges. Keeping herself occupied this way, she found that her mind remained more focused and that she worried less about what would lie ahead of her in the future.

Chapter 4
Caught

It was when the warmer days came more frequently and the colder days did not last so long, when Norah had felt something was rapidly changing at the North Pole. As she was such an expert in observing, she had started to notice that the actual time when the snow and the ice were covering the land, sea, rivers and lakes, was getting shorter and shorter. Lots of large parts of ice were coming loose from the mainland too. Many of these pieces which had come loose, started to float in the sea as far as she could see. Sometimes she found herself floating in the big sea on top of one of those big ice blocks, or 'mini-ice-islands' as she would call them. She had also noticed that some birds who used to come every year during the warmer season, did not come back as often anymore. If they did, they would not stay as long as they did before. Norah also had to start climbing higher and higher on the rock cliffs near the seaside, to find bird eggs to eat. Before these changes, she would find the bird eggs much closer to the ground. Somehow, she found it harder and harder to catch other food too.

Some bears she had met, had told Norah that they too struggled more and more with finding something to eat. These bears also looked thinner, not only in the Winter season when it was more difficult to hunt for food, but now also during the Summer season. They had told Norah that besides finding it more difficult to find food for themselves, they were really struggling to feed their young bear cubs too.

Norah was getting really worried about these changes and thought long and hard about finding solutions for them. She thought about it every day. She had come to hear about some stories from other bears who used to live at the North Pole and now lived in a forest quite a long way away. At this place other bears lived too. The bears who already lived in that place apparently had a different colour than Norah's coat. Their coat was brown and sometimes black in colour. It was said that these bears had access to plenty of food and that they lived quite happily and healthy there.

One day, after having a 'morning-swim', Norah fell asleep. When she woke up, she found herself floating in the middle of the sea, on one of those big floating ice islands. Suddenly, in the corner of her eye, she saw something she had never seen before. Norah was very curious by nature and she decided to go and investigate what she had seen. She started to swim towards it. When she managed to get near the object, she heard a lot of shouting and was suddenly surrounded by lots of ropes. She was being pulled up in the air by these ropes and by a net, which was being carried upwards by a machine of some sort. Because of her long swim, she was still quite tired and did not resist much whilst she was being caught and lifted out of the water. She was also very much in shock, as it all went so fast and sudden. Before she knew it, Norah found herself on a very large ship.

Chapter 5
Norah arrives at the zoo

Norah had seen human beings before. Sometimes she saw them not far from where she was living. These humans were often looking for food, like she was. They also caught fish at times. They used a different fishing technique than Norah did though. They used some kind of sharp tool to cut a hole in the ice, a long piece of wood, a line and some sort of sharp hook at the end, which was attached to the line. The humans would put the hook in the water and sit on the ice and wait, sometimes for a very long time, and then all of a sudden, they would pull up the wooden stick and there would be a fish attached to the hook. Norah loved watching the humans fishing that way. She liked their way of fishing, it seemed easy and fun too. She was not afraid of humans at all, although she had heard stories of other bears who were afraid of them.

This time, these humans had not caught fish - they had caught Norah. Suddenly Norah felt very sleepy too. After pulling Norah on the boat, and taking the net off her, the humans put her in a cage. After a long night's sleep, they put this cage with Norah in it, on the back of a big truck. The humans were going to take Norah to a Zoo. She could hear the drivers who were sitting in the front of the truck talk about this to each other.

Sitting, in shock, in her cage, Norah fell into a deep, deep sleep. It felt like she had slept for a very long time. When she woke up, she found herself in a hard, cold place which had a few walls and a door. It also had a little window in one of the walls which had some bars in front of it. Every so often a face would appear looking through that window. It was a face of a human being, who wanted to see how Norah was doing, to see if she was still alive.

So here she was. Norah had arrived at a zoo; it was something like a small wildlife park. After a few days, she was released from this indoor place and could go outside. There, at a distance, she saw many other bears; some black ones, brown ones but no white ones like her. It felt warm outside where she was now. It felt a bit like the Summer temperatures from where she stayed before. Where she was living now, in a small forest at the zoo, it seemed that this was the temperature for most of the year.

Many people came to see Norah and the other bears in this park. She could see the visitors from across a big pond. The humans had built the pond for her, which meant that she could have a swim and cool down a bit if she felt like doing so. She liked the pond, but it was nothing like the sea she used to swim in before. It was actually a very small pond.

Chapter 6
The Polar Bear Whisperer

There was one little boy who came to see Norah quite often at the zoo. Almost every week he was there. Norah thought he was quite a kind child as he, from a distance, to get Norah's attention, used to smile and stare at her for a very long time. He did not shout to Norah either, like many of the other children did. These children must have thought she was deaf or something. But this little boy was different. It was almost like he could hear Norah think.

She had heard of some humans, who could listen deeply and hear what animals thought and communicated about. She had heard of people having that special connection with animals. She felt that this young boy had that gift too. The funny thing was that she could also hear the little boy's thoughts. She felt a deep connection with him - it was like she could hear him whisper softly to her. She had heard of stories about children telling their worries to the animals they took care of, both to big animals such as ponies and to their pets. Talking about their problems to the animals, seemed to help these children to worry less and to build very special friendships with the animals this way.

Norah thought that if this works for children, it might also work for the animals. She decided that she was going to tell this kind and gentle boy HER story. Norah decided that she was going to tell all that had happened to her, such as where she came from and why she now lived in the zoo. She wouldn't really be 'telling' him the story but instead she would be 'thinking the story very deeply'. She hoped that the boy would hear her in his mind and would understand her, feel that same connection with her like the other children did with their befriended animals.

Every time when the little boy came to watch Norah from a distance, she would immediately spot him amongst all the other people who were visiting the zoo. The boy would always make eye contact and started to stare at Norah for a long time. The boy would always look so happy when they made eye contact and he would continue to smile at her, which made her feel happier too.

It even made her feel a little bit less sad for a while. Then she would start to think very deeply about her story and share it, only with her thoughts, with the little boy.

Norah 'told' the boy, silently with her thoughts, how she had arrived in the zoo after being caught. She shared with him, mentally, about how wonderful the place was where she used to live and how she missed being there. She 'told' him about the Northern Lights, how she missed watching the butterflies in the summer, how she dreamed of the freezing cold snow and the dazzling sparkles of the snowflakes. She also thought deeply, about how she had noticed that the freezing cold times were getting shorter and shorter and how finding food was getting more difficult. She wondered if the boy had also noticed these kinds of changes where he lives.

She told the boy with her thoughts, that these changes had made it harder to find food. The boy had a sense of calm around him, which was quite similar to the fishermen she had seen at the North Pole. These fishermen could sit there for hours sometimes, hardly moving, until they caught a fish, and then there would be great excitement of shouting and laughter. Norah thought that the boy could be a good fisherman too. He seemed to have a lot of patience whilst standing and looking at Norah, often for a very long time.

One day, when Norah was sharing her thoughts with the boy, she could suddenly hear the boy's thoughts too. First, she got a shock, and then she was so happy that she

could hear him, as this could mean that he could hear her too. His silent voice sounded like a gentle whisper: it sounded kind, inviting and understanding. Norah could hear him say that he was so sorry to hear about Norah's life story. The things Norah had shared with him that day, had made him stop smiling and Norah could see small drops of water rolling over his little cheeks. The boy suddenly looked very, very sad. Norah didn't like seeing him so upset and she started to think deep thoughts again and spoke to the boy in the silent way saying that she was so happy that they could now hear each other's thoughts. They had both discovered a 'silent' way of communication to understand each other, which was amazing and could be so helpful.

Norah wanted to give the little boy a name and called him 'The Polar Bear Whisperer'.

Norah shared with him that it saddened her to see him so upset too. She suggested to him that maybe they could form a team and 'work' together. They could tell humans about the drastic changes that were happening at the North Pole and perhaps the young boy could find out why this was happening and what could be done to stop it. They really liked each other a lot and the boy became Norah's friend and Norah became his friend.

Chapter 7
Marcin and Norah 'team - up' for the Planet

One day, 'The Polar Bear Whisperer', whose real name was actually Marcin, started to talk to his parents about his silent conversations with Norah. In the beginning, Marcin's parents did not believe Marcin at all. However, the more detailed Marcin's descriptions of the North Pole environment became, the more his parents started to wonder how on earth Marcin could know all these things about a place he had never been. Marcin had never visited the North Pole and at school they had not discussed the North Pole as a topic as such.

When they visited the zoo, they were always with Marcin and they could see that there was something special happening when Marcin looked at the polar bear. He always wanted to see her first. It was as if something magical happened between them both as they always looked so calm and focused at each other. They seemed to to have a strong connection. It really looked like they were silently communicating with each other. Marcin's parents had never witnessed such a thing in their lives. They eventually believed that Marcin and Norah had found a very special way of talking with each other.

One day, Marcin asked his parents if they knew why the ice was melting so fast at the North Pole and how it was possible that the polar bears were not getting enough food and were struggling to survive. His parents went to the village library and got some books about climate change. They also found some documentaries which they watched together on the computer. They found out that the layer of greenhouse gasses, made of water vapours, carbon dioxide, nitrous oxide, methane gasses and some other gasses, cause trapped heat. This in turn warms the Earth, like a thermal blanket. This blanket prevents these gasses to radiate from Earth to space and keeps them near the Earth instead. This is how the Earth and the seas get warmer. This is why the ice is melting so fast.

The greenhouse gasses happen for many reasons; some of them are because forests get cut down, some because of land use changes, some because of the burning of fossil fuels by cars and factories and some by the rotting of rubbish in landfill sites. Since the Industrial revolution about 200 years ago, the carbon dioxide levels in the atmosphere have increased more than three times.

These are some of the reasons why the temperature is rising on the planet and this is why the North Pole, the South Pole and the Tibetan Plateau, which some researchers call the Third Pole, are melting rapidly.

When Marcin heard about this, he asked his parents to take him to the zoo again, so he could tell Norah what he had found out about this so called 'climate change'. Marcin's parents knew by now, it was best to support Marcin on his mission to find answers for his new best friend, Norah. If they didn't support him, Marcin would not stop asking them a thousand questions about the environment and how they could solve this problem of climate change. When they would take Marcin to the zoo, Marcin and Norah would talk silently for a very long time, in their own special way, about how to find solutions for this huge problem the Earth is facing right now.

They came up with a brilliant idea. Norah and Marcin decided that from now on, every Saturday, together, they would hold a 'Question and Answer' session at the zoo. People could come and learn about climate change and the effects of it and ask questions about Norah's life at the North Pole. They could also discuss how they could help to prevent more bears struggling the way Norah had done.

During those sessions, people would ask Marcin a question and Marcin would think deeply and then 'whisper' that question, in silence, in his mind, to Norah. The people who worked in the zoo had heard about what was going on between Norah and Marcin too. At first, they didn't believe what was happening but after speaking to Marcin's parents and watching how Norah and Marcin communicated in silence, they were so amazed and excited about it that they offered a space in the zoo, for holding their Saturday meetings for the public.

This space was near the place where Norah stayed. Norah could see Marcin clearly from where she was and Marcin and the people were in safe enough distance from Norah. Everyone who came to the Saturday sessions had a seat and they all sat in a large circle and discussed solutions to prevent more damage to the Earth and to all who live on the Earth. Norah found out, during these meetings, that there were already lots of people taking action to help the Earth and the environment. She encouraged everyone, especially the children, to come up with ideas about what they could do to help even more.

Some children were talking about how they were planting trees, how they were using less electricity in their homes and how they were walking or cycling more often to school rather than their parents taking them by car. Some kids had encouraged their parents to do more about it too and to use 'green energy' or renewable energy companies for their electricity supply at their homes. Others were talking with their friends and neighbours about growing food in their villages and gardens rather than buying from big supermarkets. Some grown-ups had even written to the politicians of their country to stop polluting the Earth.

Chapter 8
Marcin and Norah need help

Marcin decided to stay a true friend to Norah and to keep helping her on her mission to protect the Earth. Norah knew that she could make a difference in the world by doing what she did, in the zoo. She was making a lot of visitors aware of the effects of global warming by telling her life-story to everyone who wanted to listen. Still to this day, thousands and thousands of adults and children continue to listen to Norah's story, told by Marcin, 'The Polar Bear Whisperer'. Norah and Marcin have both decided to continue to create awareness and to inspire people to make positive steps towards finding solutions. This is their mission in life, for the rest of their lives. To be even more successful with their mission, Norah and Marcin need your help.

They ask you to remember their incredible story, the story you just read about. It is a story about friendship, about taking care of your own and other's well-being. It is about resilience and about asking for help if you feel you need support. It is about protecting and taking care of the Earth. It is about understanding that we are all connected.

If there was one more thing that YOU could do to help look after the Earth right now, what would it be? Remember that all small changes put together, make a BIG change. After reading this story, we could even say that sometimes out of a difficult situation, like in Norah's case, something positive can happen. May our friend Norah inspire us all to always keep hope in our hearts and to create friendships wherever we are.

The End

Thank you so much! I am so pleased that you read this story, which shows that you have an interest in looking after the planet and that you are interested in the wellbeing of animals. Next time when you visit a zoo, perhaps you can start listening to the animals too, they might have something important to share with you as well.

If you know of anyone else who you think might enjoy reading this story, I hope you will pass this book on to them. - Claudia

Solution Focused Enquiry and Reflection

- What do you think about Norah's strengths?
- Could you mention at least three skills that she has that help her to overcome challenging situations?
- Are there any other qualities of Norah that you would like to point out?
- What can you say about Marcin, what qualities do you see in him?
- What did you think was the best solution that happened in this book?
- If you could mention one of your own great skills, which one would it be?
- What strength do you have that got you through a challenge in your life?
- Norah found her friend Marcin, who could help her to make people aware of the global warming situation. Who would you go to for support if you needed some?
- Who has been helpful to you in the past?
- When was the last time that you felt things were going really well for you?
- What were you doing?
- How was that helpful for you?
- What is your hope for your future?
- What are you already doing to make it happen?
- How motivated are you to follow your dreams, could you give it a number from a scale 1 to 10, ten being the highest?
- What else needs to happen to get a bit closer towards your dream coming true?
- How would you feel if your dream came true right now?
- What would you do?
- Who would notice that your dream had come true?
- What would they see in you that made them know that your dream came true?

- When was the last time you felt the same way, like your dream had come true?
- What were you doing then?
- Who was there with you?
- On a scale of 1-10, 1 being low and 10 being high, where are you now in living your dream?
- What would be happening if you were one higher up the scale?
- How confident are you on the scale, 1 being low and 10 being high, that you will make your dream come true?
- What else needs to happen for you to feel that you are on track in life?
- Who else can help you to make that happen?
- How can you help taking care of the Earth?
- Who and/or what can be supporting you in this?
- What are you already doing that is helping the environment?
- What else do you plan to do for the environment?
- What was the best part of the book for you and why?

Well done for taking the time to reflect on these questions!

You can use them again and again if you want to.

What other questions could you ask that could find solutions for climate change?

Please share them with me.

Claudia loves living on this beautiful planet and is passionate about taking good care of the Earth. Claudia is a mother and grandmother and has been working as a solution focused therapist, coach, speaker and workshop facilitator since 2002. She has given training in her own motivational, inspiring way in many countries and helps people to find meaning in their lives.

This is Claudia's first book. She believes that children are the future and that they hold the key for new innovations and ideas. She hopes that this book will inspire children to believe in their dreams and to encourage children to share their dreams with the world at large. May this book also motivate adults to support the children to fulfil their dreams and encourage children and adults to lead a purposeful life. May the story about Norah and Marcin contribute to the continuation of finding solutions for climate change and for giving children hope and inspiration to follow their dreams.

For **information** on **consultations** or **speaking seminars**, please **contact Claudia** at: solutionways@gmail.com

or you can visit her websites:

www.solutionways.com and www.consciousworldagents.com

Both, the Polar Bears and everyone else who lives on this beautiful planet, are affected by the changes we are all faced with due to climate change. Of course the planet goes through cycles anyway. However, we can all help to let the changes happen more in its natural rhythm by becoming more mindful in how we live on the planet. All our actions have an effect. Some people and animals are facing huge challenges because of the speeding up of the climate change. If you want to learn some more about Polar bears and their habitats and about people who know a lot about how to live in balance with nature, here are some websites that might be of interest to you too:

https://polarbearsinternational.org/polar-bears-changing-arctic/living-with-polar-bears

https://www.saamicouncil.net/en/home

https://ejfoundation.org/resources/downloads/EJF-Sami-briefing-2019-final-1.pdf

Printed in Great Britain
by Amazon

14918431R00025